The Art of Music
A Collection of Writings
Volume 2

Piano Press
P.O. Box 85
Del Mar, CA 92014-0085

www.pianopress.com

Published by:

Piano Press
P. O. Box 85
Del Mar, CA 92014-0085
U. S. A.

Tel: (619) 884-1401
Fax: (858) 459-3376

PianoPress@aol.com
www.pianopress.com

Printed in the United States of America

Library of Congress Control Number: 2003098418

ISBN 1-931844-12-7

PP1024

$9.95

Contents

Rasmussen, Ande - *Capture the Creative Moment*
Romond, Edwin - *Everything About Egypt, Liam and the Wichita Lineman, Mathis Sings "Maria," Piano*
Rotkowitz, Ruth - *Song of Flight*
Rudsit, Jennifer - *Discovering Joy*
Sanders, Bonny Barry - *Étude, Perfect Pitch, Sequoias*
Sedgwick, Robert - *Honky-Tonk*
Simoni, Wanda D. - *Piano*
Smith, Christopher - *Miles Davis, Rilke's Bouzouki, The Session*
Smith, Jena - *Bach for Breakfast, Ella*
Stringer, Vicki - *Closure, Philemon & Baucis Re-Incarnated in Iowa, 2000*
Taylor, Ann - *Fadista*
Thomas, Erin Alan - *Voice*
Wilshaw, Pearl Mary - *Piano Duet*

ELIZABETH C. AXFORD

My Little Brother

My little brother was a bubble of trouble
Or so he always thought, poor thing

He was plump as a child
Drove his schoolteachers wild
But jumped fleet-footed over troubled waters
He sang his own song,
Yet always tried to get along,
Still his singles got lost in the collection

We bought bubble gum
And played some, and got in trouble some
Always when it was least convenient for Mom & Dad
Like that one time right before that party they had

He would follow me to town
When he hadn't any friends around,
And I'd try to protect him
And when we got older,
We would argue more often
Because the friend we had in each other
Had been taken over by some other

We did things differently,
Especially Right & Wrong
He always wanted to participate,
I never wanted to sing along
Like during our school years, poor thing

Then I got my wedding ring,
And he said, "Good bye"
Oh, what I would have given
To let the tear drain from my eye
And my heart fell
For I knew the time with my little brother was gone

Yes, he had his own song
Still he tried to sing along
And every year he would buy the

Family a Christmas present
As if to say, "I like this family, can I please stay?"

He was always a part,
Always, from the start,
Yet so tenderly he tried to be a member
For this our little brother
We will always cherish and remember

RONALD K. BURKE

In Jazz There is Unity

You can imagine my surprise when I heard the
sounds of jazz in the air at a flea market
You can imagine my surprise when I heard wiggle
like a snake and waddle like a duck suddenly
transform into a jazz riff.

You can imagine my happiness to discover at the end
of a row of concessions a mellow musical bouillabaisse
wending its way in the warm sunny air by virtue of a
tall dark greyheaded figure playing a mellow mellow
tenor sax a cool cool seriously exotic electric guitarist a
busy busy drum drumming drummer and an eloquent
clearly articulate bassist cooking up a gentle riot.

You can imagine my sense of inner pride knowing I
belonged to a special kind of cool club as I sat in a
folding chair with one or two other aficianados at my
side who looked to be disciples straight out of the
fifties and sixties while many squares ignorant of the
creativity being wrought right in their midst zombied
on by our miniscule gathering.

You can imagine my enjoyment as I grooved along
with my new found devotees to Bye Bye Blackbird.
The tenor in his cool Coltrained-like passion and his
fierce harmonic imagination the guitarist with his
wit and magnificent dexterity the drummer and his
imaginative percussion and the tremulous effect of
the bass which added a pleasant feel to the gifted
ensemble made for a sensational afternoon.

Think about it--jazz enthusiasts can travel anywhere and music's language brings us together. In jazz there is unity.

MARIANNA BUSCHING

At St. Cecelia's Window

In the gray medieval gloom
where summer-shaded stones still
hoard a thousand winters' chill
stands St. Cecelia's pillared room,

her leaded portrait cut in white
and amber glass. The frozen strings
stretched on her crystal lute ring
silent melodies of light.

Her fixed and parted lips still send
upwards the mute and glowing chants
heard just by Heaven's occupants
where ranked and tiered burning choirs
stroke their incandescent lyres
and join her stanzas without end.

STEPHEN BUTTERMAN

Piano Sonata Seen

Tumble in windy
swerves of
candles flickering
O dancing light on dusty
Books, O waltz in
…time…
to coffee's opulent
aroma
think of
(nothing but)
forgetting
Leaves–leaves thoughts
Fluttering
in candle winds

d
  o
w
  n
to cushioned contentment
and sway–sway thoughtless
  painless
    weightless
with me
for Now

LORAINE CAMPBELL

Silent Way
Miles horn
and Davis hands
caress that
blow that yearns,
that horn
that burns,
skipping notes
and thumping hearts
wrack my back
with torn apart.
Miles of Davis,
miles of road,
highways, road
signs–way to go!
Eerie travel
through my soul,
silent Miles
day to know.

FERN G. Z. CARR

Cool Jazz
A curl of thin blue smoke
snakes around a half empty glass
of stale scotch,
and as the ice cubes melt,
the lazy swooshing of a brush
caresses percussion cymbals;

The mellow plucking
of thick strings on the double bass
is in counterpoint
with the twang of an electric guitar
and the pained expression
on the guitarist's face;
While sultry saxophone
romances the house,
confident fingers fly
across the keyboard -
pianist, eyes closed,
sways back and forth
entranced by the rhythm he creates,
shoulders heaving
as he makes love to the piano -
It's jazz and it's cool baby; uh huh.

TODD CECIL

Time Signature
I found the notes
Collected in the attic
Cleaning out my grandfather's life
They were brass
And some made of strings
And some had voices from the sky
Surely one time looked upon as stars
They were all hidden under a noisy surface
Like Picassos under scratched glass
And there I sat interpreting
The 40's and 50's with 78's
Black and spinning like a clock
Turning hands back
To a time that I could hold on to
A place where the walls were made of music
And sounded like so many rooms
That time had abandoned
And there in this room
Down inside the mahogany player
I found my grandfather
Vibrant in his youth
Finding a way back

With hair black and shiny
Like his shoes
I revisited times
And places I had never been
And in things past
And darkened out
It dawned that death
Never steals a memory
It just displaces it
Into the time of music

LAURA COBRINIK

To a Street Musician

"You stand there
with your violin—
The score looks
pasted to *the Wall.*
A little blonde boy
holds his favorite toy.
He studies you
with awe."

"Where do you serenade your violin?"

"Are you on a street
in Brooklyn, New York,
Brooklyn, Mississippi,
Chicago, Los Angeles,
San Antonio, or are you
in Jerusalem playing for
Peace at the Western Wall?"

"What do you perform on your violin?"

"Do you perform
the classical mode,
music of:
Chopin, Mozart, Bach;
Or, the folk-pop music,
the love ballads of:
The Beatles, the Carpenters,

or Springsteen?"

"Or, do you perform
the fun-and-fancy tunes,
the Hora and circus carousel tunes;
Or, do you perform the *laaahh–*
baaahh-daahh-da-dadaaah,
heart-aching, crying-feeling
music of the soul—
Klezmer tunes,
that take me back home to the Shtetl?"

"Tell me, *Street Musician*
where or what do you perform?
For whom do you make music?"
"With your back turned

I'm not sure if you're glad or sad,
but I do hope that your melodies
pray for World Peace—Shalom!"

DEBORAH A. DESSASO

Fluegelhorn
A jazz band in the Great Hall
at noon.

A man from the brass section
saunters
from the back row
to the front,

lifts to his lips
a horn formed
when a trumpet
and cornet crossed paths,
clashed, then cleaved
into a fluegelhorn.

The sultry whine of the horn's notes
lifts
my heels, and for a moment

I'm in the dentist' chair
listening to the office radio
playing cool jazz
through the muffled haze of Twilight Sleep. . .

Play that song, jazz man,
one   more   time.

The Tuning ♫ 2002 Second Place Winner

A performance on short notice.

Two girls.

A mother, unshaken
by pouts or sullen looks.

A violin. A cello.

A music teacher on the other
side of town.

A speakerphone, its volume
button   slid
to the max.

Echoes of the scale
followed by the teacher's
voice squawking instructions:

Let me hear that E…
Too flat…
Play it again…
Again…
Now the F…
Too sharp…
Again…
Now you're ready.

The voice and the finger
that tune by
speakerphone can bring
order from chaos.   Really.

<u>JIM DEWITT</u>

<u>On-Tour Harmonica Man</u>

On-tour harmonica man
sips at his notes, pretending to be
a second-string orchestra . . .
audience ears
accustomed to being oiled
can appreciate his cough-like riffs –
c'mon, build thirst for squeals
of a sun-drenched beach
or sentimental stabs at
the wayward winds –
and flying music to ring around birds
bailing out of trees . . .
or perfume bottles foaming
like soda pop –
now he knows his listeners will follow
to wherever that vibrating throat can pied-piper them

<u>GELIA DOLCIMASCOLO</u>

<u>Danse Poetica</u>

The dancer weaves
          body through space
The poet reveals
          words on paper
Both spin the thread
          of human spirit
Neither seeks completion
          but passage
The dancer weaves
          a poem for today
The poet dances
          a song for tomorrow

<u>MARY E. DUNCAN</u>

<u>Tony's Mandolin</u>

Once more,
The old man
Takes the mandolin,

And holds it close.
Then,
A pause,
A caress.
An unwhispered prayer,
And with his soul
At high pitch!
Bends the strings
With sounds so pure!
Angels rush to listen,
And each note tells him,
He is young again.

ELAINE ERICKSON

Between Concerts *(for Beth Lawrence)*
Your soprano voice meanders
like sunlight. A bare
light bulb penetrates the stage
and you're behind the curtain,
warming up with Bach
under your breath, waiting
to transform the light bulb
to chandeliers. The silence
after the music
is a hovering ghost.

Cancer hits you like lightning—
an explosion of glass in your breast.
The doctor throws out a new word:
a mastectomy. You hear
a lone bird whistling
in the branches. Your life
is a cup of sparkling water
half drunk, your years
gliding by like fragile boats.

You know what you must do.
You must sing under the doctor's
knife—sing Verdi's Aida,
The Lord's Prayer.
As the doctor probes, his blade

glittering moons, you sing
with the power of horses hooves
pounding through morning's
slate gray stillness.

DAVID FAGEN

Waiter, the Check Please

Shrill co-untry music smites the air
With cheatin' bleatin' low-down fare
Ear-drums and taste buds wince and clash
Cole Porter tunes – a thing long past
The menu caviar to prime rib rare
The music frays raw nerves threadbare
The lyrics scream a single theme
A never-ending carnal fling:

"Forgive me darlin' Cindy Lou
T'was wrong of me for lovin' you
While married to your mother Fay
I shoulda never run away
But I'm a bird who must fly free
I hope you name the kid for me."

Song follows song, each song the same
The beat, the melody, the sobbed refrain
Guitars cry out, the voices wail
'He-She-They' tried so hard but failed

The food first-rate, the service great
Let's get out of here, it's getting late
Enough of cheatin' low-down fare
Where co-untry music smites the air

MARDELLE FORTIER

Composing Poems as Music Plays in a Coffee House

Satin of imagination
    so liquid, so lovely
    musical silk

Trails of fantasy

dance in saxophone
scallops around my neck
throbbing neck

Pianissimos glitter in
glissandos on ephemeral sleeves
Sleek chords glove me, silvery
flutes crown me, fall over
my eyes in a teasing veil

Drums stitch the orchestral fabric
tighter to waist, to thigh, to foot
Sliding notes become part of me

I can never stop caressing
satin seven times more lush
more lyric
more real
than my own skin

Katerina Witt Competes
Katerina—bullets in her eyes
lipstick red as the edge of a knife

brain on a cool and vigilant watch
ready to snap shut.

Yet after competitors sit down
and she skates out on the ice flying

she dances flowing with the gold refrain
of the mellifluous, muscled violin

she floats inside the yearning of each note
married to each shade and shape of it

she leaps as the music towers over her
glides with limbs stretched like a dancer.

Only when the singing comes to rest
does she end with an elegant satiny twist.

Listening to Jazz in the Coffee House

Piano like breaking glass
spills across my vitals,
shining glass. I thought I was safe,
here with my coffee. I thought
I was free from memory. No, the notes
crashed across my breast, opened
a long-ago remembrance.
So many high keys; tiny fragments
of glass—and my heart
breaks in pieces because it is
only the size of a vase.

Perfect Pair ♫ 2003 First Place Winner

Dancing as one
turning as one
they are slender
and dressed in black
2 musical notes expanding
covering silent ice
He glides while she spins
Both bodies form a line
straight and silken
when he holds her above him

With soaring hearts of Slavic fire
they stay in rhythm
fly higher
He lifts her fluidly as a violin
As music they defy
for the moment
time and gravity
He stands motionless
a dark quarter note
on a white page while she pirouettes
Their pale arms extend
with harmonious yearning
He arabesques with her
and their great pulses synchronize

Like music
they are ceaseless and perfect

down to the last
spiral of death

(for Katya Gordeeva, who paired with Sergei Grinkov to win the highest skating prizes in the world…until after his heart attack at age 28, she was left a young widow)

Skater to "Red Violin"
(A poem dedicated to Michelle Kwan)
The skater spins in a velvet blur
of reddish-gold.
Ice stretches out for her
long and cool.
Violin beats inside the chords
of the skater's neck.
Her image is adagio, her feet
are infinite.

She's stepped out of a case and glides for us
across the frost.
As the ice sings, with a glowing soul
we forget we are dust.
A lone dream yearns at the heart
of the song;
she dances with the music
as it longs gold tresses stream
Above her and within her.
Fluid as music, as hope or pain or joy
the skater flies in the air.

Her heart is flying to a place
of secret carmine.
We're left with the mirror less beauty
of a lonely violin.

G. G. GILCHRIST

inexpressible is music
Bliss (Definable? Is 'poem'?),
  as sparks through psyche, stars through soulscape's
   scrim-set northern lights,
   then breathless dopplered

in earphoned codas, mellow-muted
  privacies in paradise…

Sounds, more than culled vibrations
 (from airs invisible to insights
  surfing solitude's
  websites?), wing wonders;
or, liquid living languages, learned
  through osmosis of mind's moods…
Sonic gifts your musics' tapes
 for looping my resonating calms
  in contemplations'
  explorations through
soul's geologies, geographies,
  astronomies: worlds within…

Treasured bliss you've troved for me
in sundown-haven's blest hermitage
  where I'm seed-sowing
  fancies' fruits, (fancied?)
legacies, lately harvested verse,
  lyrics for echoes later…

Twin Solos? Duets!
Your woman's advice
   may sometimes sound unfinished,
      proclaims Spanish proverb.
But you'd prove fool, sir,
   impudent ignoramus,
      should you 'dis'/miss her wiles.
Dancers? Guitarists?
   Each, swapping roles in songstreams,
 musics, movements mellows…
Daily in duets,
   two mind-meld both heads to hearts,
 lip-synching treble, bass…
While time's metronomes
  spirits-chordings synthesize,
    'improv' molds melodies…
Re-tuned, solo scores
  of lover's lyrics, life's lilts,
     play out polyphonic….

HOWARD GOLD

Dancing

From a barn dance to a square dance
From a movie set to the Rockettes
In a foreign land or on American Bandstand
Dancing has been with us for a long time
There was Fred and Ginger, and Gene Kelly too
Even Gregory Hines has graced the pines
from 42nd Street to Saturday Night Fever to
Dirty Dancing, there's always a flick about
strutting your stuff.
Even Dorothy clicked her heels together in the
Wizard of Oz!
The variety of dances would even make Baskin Robbins
stand up and take notice!
There's the polka, lindy, and foxtrot too
Twist, tango, and the hullabaloo!
To name a few!
Get out your tap shoes, and click your heels
together. No! We're not going to Kansas!
We're just going to burn off some calories at the local disco.
So get in step, and let the spirit move you!
It's a little bit funky, and a little bit rock n roll
but always a swingin' good time!

PETER GRIMALDI

Piano Dust

She saved pennies and dimes for years
Each coin a week of her youth
To afford the one thing she desired
A piano to play music
Which her parents could not afford.
The day came, she had the music delivered,
And for months she played and played,
Until the final music was played for her
The piano now sits,
gathering dust rather than music.

Piano Moving

Five came to take away my mother's music.

Her piano, elderly, 1913 built and
Worth twenty-five dollars,
I secretly played it once, like a child trying to open
Christmas packages too early and discovered
it needed tuning.
She would tell stories of the 1929 depression days
and saving money for music,
She died in '75. Never heard her play.
I stood silent as they took away my Mother's music.

<u>St. Joseph's Piano</u>
The dragging day of university classes now dead,
To read I sat in a quiet corner of the student center
In a large antique chair comfortable from time
And use by so many others, just me, Hesse and coffee.
Then entered another blue jean and sweatshirt decorated student
Sitting at the piano located in the center of the center
And he played.
Without announcement, introduction or apology for arresting silence
or causing music to break the peace,
And he played.
Harsh fluorescent light became soft, all students ceased studies
and gathered like scientists in Kubrick's 2001: Space Odyssy film,
the scene on the moon around the black object.
We all watched and ate the music in silence until
For whatever reason the student stopped,
Stood and left the building.
He had played.

<u>ANITA GROSSMAN</u>

<u>Piano Teacher</u>
Let's see now—what great talents must I see today?
Ah, yes—Natasha with the long curls, and the mother.
Wish she'd leave Mama at home!

Eugenia. . . here she is now. . . time to start my day.
I wish that Elsa'd bring my mail.
Eugenia didn't practice, I can tell.
There's no improvement in the Mozart.
She did it this well—or badly—last week!

Good time to read my mail. Ah! Here it is! Dear, lovely Elsa.
I'll put it on the other piano and peruse it
while Eugenia struggles at the keyboard.
I wonder if she's up to handling a concerto.
We must do all the Mozarts on the radio.

Perhaps this plum would be a good incentive.
The promise (or the fear?) will make her practice more.
Yes, what a puff-up that would be—
performing a concerto by Mozart on the radio!

MICHELLE GUNNING

Old Friend, Piano
While busy complicating
life
Piano calls, come
play
The dusty keys offer to
please
A weary soul for
rest
See the old forgotten
friend
That stands and waits
asking
Shall we play together
today?
Approaching with gentle touches of
tunes
So dust lifts gradually
away
We play with cautious
care
Discussing life's present sorrows,
tests
Reflect on memories
shared
Of distant times at frequent
play
when we were young and
free

<u>KATHLEEN GUNTON</u>

<u>In Tune</u>
Do not let minor keys
make you sad, or soft-
pedal a polka. No one
can dance while you
work, anyway. Quiet helps.
Like you the ivory
is centered with ***C***.
It makes music easy
to read but there is a range
below and octaves higher.
Weather plays with music.
Strings stretch, wood expands.
Now it is time for hands.
Bring the black attaché closer.
First remove the action.
You know where
to rest the tools,
how far to turn them.
This is what you do. Begin.
Good piano tuners always
hear beats in the air.

<u>PEGGY C. HALL</u>

<u>Taps, Reveille, Taps</u>
(For September 11, 2001)

Here's to you,
in your graves.
Though we weep, may you rest, may you know
that our love
surges on
like the waves.

Though dark is the day and nearby is night,
We blazon our lights to their brightest.
Through virtue of truth and trust in our God,
We shake off the shrouds of sleep.

We wake, rise up, move forward
As drums and trumpets speak.
Fired-up, hearts flame hot, burn strong,
Justice is what we seek.

And to you,
in your graves,
though we weep, may you rest, may you know
that our love
surges on like the waves.

JOSEPH HART

Music
I lie alone at 5 o'clock
And listen to the sounds
Of darkness and he stereo
And Mendelssohn and Bach.

And all my stomach, all my soul
Receptively respond
And trenchant feel the things I hear;
And all the room is whole.

I hear nocturnal music play
And in my gut I feel
The pleasure more articulate
Than in the light of day.

a picture found in an old book of music
Chiaroscuro cherubs in ensemble
Dance among the heather with their trumpets
Clashing small grey cymbals in the silence
While night boils black and whitely from the heath.
A sylvan nymph stands near the lightning-roses
And blows her bleak recorder in the twilight.
Pale limp narcissus and warm edelweiss
Hang loosely in her shadow-hair. The moon
Drops petals to pale and silver pool
That's unreflecting like a darkened mirror.
Four naked cherubs link their tiny hands
And dance a brief quadrille among the leaves.

The grass is darkness crushed. A rhythmed fog
Obscures the silent music of the scene.

JOHN R. HAWS

My Music
There are these sounds within my head
that long to be expressed somehow.
There are these rhythms in my blood.
They move, they flow, with each breath now.

Some harmonies, some melodies,
some transitory phrases,
little bits of this and that
as I live through various phases.

I don't know why they are in me,
I only know they are to Be.

They come. They go. They hang around.
They seem to mellow more with age.
They strike the very heart of me
with a mild, contented sort of rage.

It's poetry, pure poetry,
this must do music thing
that vibrates through time and space
and makes my soul sing.

DERRYL R. HERRING

The Loom
A harp of cedar stands,
Its strings of white against a turquoise sky,
While fingers spin majestic colors
Into threads of loving harmony.

Its strings of white against a turquoise sky,
The loom stands patiently, and waits
While fingers improvise on harmony
With geometric melody.

The loom awaits the loving hands
Of one whose heart holds mysteries
Of geometric melody and harmony,
With dancing rhythms for the eye.

One whose heart holds mysteries
Kneels before a cedar harp,
Weaving threads of rhythm, melody, harmony
With finger-spun majestic hues.

Morning

In the brief interlude
          Between darkness and dawn,
Time stops for a moment
          To rest;
No wind in the piñons,
No whispering streams,
No singing of birds
          In their nests.

The light of the sun
          Finds its way through the dark
And touches the orient door.
I wake from my sleep,
All nestled in wool.
I rise from my bed
          On the floor.

I am called to the door.
          Shimá says
"My child, come here
          and we'll sing to the sun."
So we face the east
And welcome the light,
Then off through the desert I run.

I fly like a bird
          Over piñon and sage,
As naked and free
          As the wind.
Then homeward I turn
To hogan and fire.

It's time for the day
To begin.

(*Shimá* in the Navajo language means *my mother*.)

Morning Sun
Morning sun filters through the hogan door,
And I wake.

Father's voice beckons me, I stretch and yawn,
And we run.

Side by side through the piñon, over sage,
Father, son

Greet the dawn, running over Mother Earth
Like the wind.

Morning sun reaches out to touch my face,
And I sing.

KATHRYN B. HULL

Music…
that sometime sound,
that elusive rhythm
which comes from deep
within the human soul
and makes the spirit sing
expressing joy, sadness,
love, loneliness,
pain, pleasure,
but mostly
Self.

that language which
speaks without words,
that movement which
encompasses all of nature,
all of life,
giving shape
to illusive patterns,

but mostly to
Self.

This is music to me.

RICHARD KENNISON

Piano Man
Two hands ten fingers
Juggle eighty-eight hot keys—
Tip jar full of air.

SUSAN LANDGRAF

Music Sculpture Garden After the Legacy of Bandmaster George Ives
Here in the garden, the horns;
there on the rooftop
the drums
and the strings among
the birches,
flautist by the pond
sitting on a metal chair.

Visitors walk through
the sounds, as if
trouble wasn't waiting,
as if they were traveling
into the notes
waiting to be made
into concert.

A Jew's harp filters
the elm leaves
"in the sweet by and by" and
"nearer my God to"
the birches,
the dandelions,
the humming Cosmos.

Potted Tulips
His fingers
strain

to keep
up,

another
note

and another,
the dark

room
humming

at the edge.
He sinks

into
a note

and another
invented

spring,
the tulips

bending
their stems,

their heads
open.

<u>JAMES LIPSKY</u>

<u>Music is a Lot of Fun</u>
Don't slide on the trombone
Don't jump on the drums
Don't walk on the piano
Music's not this kind of fun

Don't clobber the cymbals
Don't sit on the sax
Don't fiddle with the fiddles
Don't turn the volume to max, 'cause…

Music is a lot of fun
Listen 'til the day is done
Notes can walk or they can run
Yes, music's fun for everyone

You can dance or you can rest
Whatever makes you feel the best
Listen under moon or sun
Yes, music is a lot of fun

LISA STOKKING LUTWYCHE

Orchestra Brat

backstage again
I am a little girl
waiting
for my Daddy
to come in
from that glittering
magical place
beyond the litter
of black cases

waiting
in the gentle
easy chatter
of stagehands
who feel like family

backstage
in the green room
(that is indeed green)
I am a child
again

the music coming
flawless
to the wooden bench
where I sit,
primly,
with my sisters
(in our patent leather

shoes)
bathing in Brahms

backstage
I am a scrawny
college kid
hanging
between classes
and symphonies
to catch a train
with Dad

who bursts
through crowds
with
turquoise twinkle eyes
and
an unrelenting stride
(which I match)

now, backstage
I am a woman
waiting for lunch
with my father

we will eat sushi
and speak of my children
and my half brothers
(four terrific kids,
alike in mischief,
alike in
capabilities)
and we will laugh
until tears tickle
in the corners
of our matched set
of
aqua eyes
while the music
hangs,
dancing,
in the air

MARK MANSFIELD

Für Elise

Like softest rain,
        two next-door notes
                begin this way,
a little song
        that students once
                all learned to play.
Written for
        a girl, they say,
                he barely knew,

tonight my hands,
        from memory,
                play it for you.

The Surf Aces

The Surf Aces play here tonight,
though now it's only half past five
but nice and cool in this old dive.

Each stool's still stacked but one barfly's,
whose glass is never less than half
empty of its strange dark draught.

Once more he rolls a pair of dice
upon the bar, then barely lifts
his glass. Meanwhile, his weak eye drifts,

as always, down at the two scratched eyes
staring up at his, which seem assuaged
by the empty club and its darkened stage.

No one stops in to patronize
this old night spot. Except for him,
the place is dead; the lights are dim.

The Surf Aces play here tonight,
though now it's only half past five
but nice and cool in this old dive.

<u>Wonderful World</u>
*Don't know much about . . .*Sam Cooke

Sometimes a song hits you mid stride.
Like "Wonderful World." No, not
Sam Cooke's original, but a swell cover
done of it by Herman's Hermits.

Hermits' drummer, ex-hairdresser
Barry Whitman just rides
one cymbal for all he and it have got
through almost all the guitarist's

break, making me think what better
nonsense is there, as it's
off to the races, now, my smart ass caught
by Barry and his cymbal's wild

ringing. Some songs, they never miss.
Who knows much more than this?

<u>DAVID NAPOLIN</u>

<u>Appalachian Spring</u> ♫ 2002 Third Place Winner
The hills rise under the sun
And the trees murmur with their young leaves.
Small shoots dot the ground,
The crocuses already here.

Round the faded shanty homes
Small plots, squares of broken soil,
Are seeded for the meager meal.
Barefoot children on the rising grass
Skip and jump to feel the new warmth.

Mountains in the distance
Loom large, spreading height
In hearts of the simple folk.
Snow still shines aloft.

The cold is memory stored.
The old songs rise again.

The birds trill again.
A soft wind breathes
As life relives again.

Maine Morning
In me, the stillness of the shore
the fullness of the lake
the light swinging over the water
above the tremor of wave
amid silence and space
the wholeness of the sky.

I shall shout against its void
up, into its purity
pushing my voice and longing into its depth.
For sweet is the sound of the wave
the pulse of the heart's rising song
my oneness with the wind.

Nightfall
The evening nods with easy grace,
Lower and lower from the western sky.
Velvety blues lie along the sidewalk,
Lean against the walls of buildings,
Touch the windows, and slowly sink
Into the alleys to sleep in darkness. . .
A winter tree shadows the ground,
and telephone wires stave the sky with unsung music.
The street lights in a slow crescendo
Ignite the evening.

SHARI O'BRIEN

A Debutante
Somehow, the laugh lines and crow's feet
on the exquisitely carved quaint face
of the upright centenarian
never crinkled at me before that day
I first returned her curtsey.

She made no new or grand entrance,
as she'd lived there within the cabinet

for years she managed to defy,
and countless times she had sung to me
through a perfect set of ivory teeth,
a bit tawny now, but still intact,
my hands pressing them, in fact,
ten thousand times when I took the credit
for her virtuosity.

But on that day, I watched, abashed,
her neat black patent leather-clad feet dance,
still and always like a debutante,
and thought, *dare I make it a duo?*

And so, our hearts pounding,
we spun around and around,
I in my worn blue jeans,
and she in her best oak gown.

HANS OSTROM

Bobby's Crop ♬ 2003 Third Place Winner
Bobby leased two-hundred acres,
planted clarinets & saxophones. Come harvest
time, he hired bands to play them. It's a good life,
farming instruments. Folks say
even Bobby's pigs root rhythmically.
His cows chew the blues.
Oh that sweet Kansas breeze,
swagging through sugar beets and wheat—
and catfish nosing into dusky
muck. That
tornado shuffling up I-35 from Oklahoma
—ain't no thing to Bobby.
It skirts his acres, sniffs the barn,
now doglegs to Nebraska.
Bobby calls the twister Coltrane, goes
inside, fetches iced tea for himself
and the Missus, plenty of sugar
and a downbeat of lemon. *Hey, Bobby.*

Interior Departments
I am the Minister of Leaves who writes memos in re:

deciduous policy. I strike compromises
between the forest and the trees.

Someone in the Ministry is singing a song,
a green song as insistent and calm as
succulent leaves in the Amazon Basin.

I am promoted beyond bureaucracies
of my own beliefs, am carried
on melody to ancient stands of timber.

The Lesson

Open your mouth and sing. Invisible birds
of fate will fly out and migrate toward the end
of your life. No one knows from where song
springs. Origins hide in subsequencies.
The present is the only traceable source
of song. Open your mouth. Sing.

The song may start from memory, if not
there then from tongue, throat—
or from rhythmic knees, swaying
hips, percussive rain. Perhaps from
predicament, which we call heart, or
from soul, which is history ingested.
Open. Sing. Whatever sound you have

is what you have to add to the big noise of
now for now. Nobody's listening but someone
may hear. Maybe nothing will come out
except invisible birds. Nothing is a hell
of a song, too. Zen blues—in the key of zero,
which stands for open, which is how mouth
tells noise it's time to go on, get out there,
mix it up in this concert hall, the air.

BARBARA PELMAN

You Can't Play Music With Your Head

It's time you stopped your defeatist attitude,
took on the challenge, let go of all the strife
It's time you breathed yourself into your flute

and made it sing your song, your own full life.

You can't play music only with your head,
you can't control each motion and each sound:
your fingers know their places, know the spread
of skin on silver; let the notes be found

through body's intuition, thought by heart
and felt by mind, a silent singing cry—
what's known in cell and tendon, that's the art
to let it flow through empty body's sigh.

It's time, he said. A time of letting go—
coming to the yes, forgetting no.

WANDA PODGORSKA-RUSSELL

Milton's Music
Sitting in Krakatoa Café in Fresno,
reading to Milton "Ride Sally Ride,"
two musicians singing
to the brush of drumsticks and a flute,
"—corn' on, come on and ride, ride,
jump on, jump on and ride the pony,"
their voices wind around the room,
my foot is tapping,
Sampson Agonistes just pulled down
the pillars and Milton is silent,
listening to "Ride Sally Ride."

CHARLES RAMPP

music teacher
she's like a good, tight roof
which gets no daily praise,
          or even thought.
I've heard her sing and play
a thousand children into music heaven,
discovering wonders
        of their own creativity.
gentle voice is warm with joy
as out-of-tune church basement piano

becomes a cosmic surf board
for a dozen notable children.
    no matter that mallets fell
on wrong bars of xylophone,
some rhythms were loosely followed,
or a bow dragged on strings,
lips loosened at a mouthpiece
and squeaks whistled from soft reeds —
smiles and encouragements never failed
    as she quietly discovered
and extended (always)
    their limits of performance

singer
no worlds of life orbit our blue planet,
as hot or cold – dead to organized hearts,
the others spin.

your joy unchallenged lives
in the same light
which would be quite lonely,
except that we follow like comet's trail
or meteor swarm.
                        Lady,
sing us home
to fall as tribute fire,
untouched stage-thrown flowers,
quiet,
        hoping for white hands.

ANDE RASMUSSEN

Capture Your Creative Concepts
Capture your creative concepts before they float away!
Like green and purple helium balloons let go on a windy day!
The greatest minds in history have written what they thought,
There's many others who could have been great,
they got the thought, didn't jot, then forgot.
If they had written it down or at least had something to write,
Their futures would be clear and ridiculously bright,
The next time an idea arrives, be ready and record,
Many lives can change from a few scribbled words.

The secret is so simple, it's quite easy to overlook,
Just keep as your companion a pen and a blank book!

EDWIN ROMOND

Everything About Egypt ♫ 2003 Second Place Winner

for Sister Judith

Music was only supposed to last
from 12:20 to1 but
on St. Patrick's Day Sister Judith
seemed radiant as star dust
clover so on we sang
holding the geography of Egypt
for another day. I remember
our forty-two faces lighting
with Sister's love for the songs
of Ireland that afternoon Egyptian
rivers had to wait while Vito
Carluzzi crooned, "When Irish
Eyes Are Smiling" and Stash
Jankowski belted "Me Father's
Shillelagh." We just kept singing
and singing with the pyramids and
sphinxes growing one day older
for soon it was 1:30, then it was 2
in a room filled with fifth graders
and a nun we loved being one
voice beautiful as prayer. And I,
like a lucky leprechaun, found
a pot of gold in the second row
where pretty Jane Ellen Hughes
sang "O Danny Boy" and I dreamed
in green she was really singing
"O Eddie Boy" as we walked hand
in hand along a Galway shore.
So, Sister Judith, lovely lady of God,
know that this boy in the back
remembers when we kept text books
closed to spend all afternoon in song
and that joy is an emerald river
flowing through my soul and forty years
later I need to thank you for everything

about Egypt we did not learn the day
you let the lesson plan go, one March 17th
when none of us could stop the music.

Liam and the Wichita Lineman

Liam wiggles like a terrified fish
when I lift him from his cradle at 3 a.m.,
his tears dot my pajama top and I
don't have a clue about what to do
to soothe him. So maybe it's some male-
bonding muse from the 60's that prompts me
to sing the soft loneliness of "Wichita Lineman"
to my week old son who knows already
the pain of waking to nothing more
than the grin on his Big Bird night light.

I feel necessary as love here
in the dark of the nursery with Liam clinging
with frantic hands and, if I had words
he could understand, I'd tell him how good
it is go be a man and cry for someone.
But all I can do is whisper "Wichita Lineman"
and hope a song about needing and wanting
for all time can ease him back to sleep. Then
because it seems the right thing to do,
I begin to waltz with my son around the cradle

and his voice turns quiet as my slippers
on the carpet. I'm telling him about another man,
one of us alone on phone pole in Kansas,
whose hands clutch cable in the sky,
yearning perhaps for some of this peace
that grows within me dancing
with my newborn boy whose feet sway
like a wire in the wind till he falls asleep
against my chest, his tiny breath a life
line wrapping around and around my heart.

Mathis Sings "Maria"

and
two
lovers

boiling
in
youth
touch
tongues
between
fire
escape
rails
and
yearn
for
some
where
as
two
stars
cross
above
the
moon
grieving
in
the
west
side
sky.

Piano

It's only polished darkness in our living room
until Mary let the music out.
I can't name one note on what she loves
and I've learned there's little
I can do to make her eyes light
as much as when she's touching the keys
into music. Sometimes on summer nights
I have seen neighbors stand in the street
listening to the music from her hands
and now, our young son sits on her lap
as she plays Beethoven around him.
I love the mystery of her fingers finding melody
where I see only black and white. I love her

smile as she follows the notes
for she knows how grateful I am
that, on my own, this Baldwin piano
would sing only silence but, because of her,
our home is filled with the rapture of song.

RUTH ROTKOWITZ

Song Of Flight

How can I ever let go?
Open my fist to the wind,
Let the crumpled leaf fly away?
Humming that bursts from my hand
Now grows distant
A melody I do not know
Soaring to the skies.
What will become of me,
My days, my nights,
The songs we sang together,
Our sweet harmony
Back and forth?
Two slippery smooth shells at the beach
Shiny, opalescent pink-white,
One buzzing with the ocean's tunes
Eager to follow the whooshing water's chords,
Sailing out
High on the waves.
Another
Coated with sticky sand,
Sinking deeper and deeper
The music of the sea fading.

Can it be
That the child's leaving
Fills the mother with emptiness and fear
And – maybe
Space
For a new tune?

<u>JENNIFER RUDSIT</u>

Discovering Joy

At seven-years-old
I was marching up the steps
to Mrs. Jones' house,
piano flashcards digging
into my palms, when what
I wanted was to be a gymnast
tumbling on the blue and white
mats, learning cartwheels,
walkovers, and backflips.

But I was too tall, too tall,
too tall. I pulled my skirt
down a little, over my spindly
legs and rang her doorbell.
I knew where middle C was,
that my practice book seemed
to love songs about Indian maidens
and red hens, and that treble clef
was played with the right hand.

After three years,
the only thing I could play
was the junior version
of Beethoven's symphony 9
and only with the right hand.
That year my parents sold
the piano to another mother
whose unsuspecting daughter
would learn the rigors of music.

But now, whenever I come upon
an empty piano, I sit and slowly
run my fingers back and forth
over the keys, remembering
those chords, that symphony.

BONNY BARRY SANDERS

Étude

Today she practices her flute
on our patio. I pretend
not to listen. Does she realize
she is the soloist

in an orchestra
of killdeer, crickets, meadowlarks,
mockingbirds, some early cicadae?
At first, she thinks only of the challenge

to her position as first chair. Her notes
ascend in a slur of triplets, a legato
the late afternoon can accept. Out
in the fields a sparrow hawk hovers

as if listening before diving to his prey.
The tops of the cedar trees by the fence
flicker like candles lit by rays
of light. Then with an allargando

of whole notes, she counts the sun down.
She's found new meaning for unison.
She is listening. She echoes the trills
of the meadowlarks.

She holds on to each phrase like a trust,
then enters her own cadenza
that wings out beyond bar lines
with the freedom of flight.

Her aria cantabile will go nameless.
She does not care; today she has broken
through to a new truth—
improvisation will be the god of her art.

Perfect Pitch

I'd leave the closet door
open. A yellow square
of light on the closet floor

from the laundry chute to the basement
 soaked our room
  though my fears only grew.

Feather pillows exhaled their breathy weight
 like the heavy rhythm of my lungs.
  I'd lie on my top bunk; my little brother

slept below. I dared not move or test
 the murky recesses of the room—
  every thud or creak from the old house

warned of crawling things that would find me.
 The smell of steam from Mother's iron
  on damp clothes escaped

through the bright square. The rhythmic click,
 the push of the iron and her soft hum
  struck up a shove and push, shove and push,

shuss of steam on slightly frayed trousers
 worn at the cuff, hiss
  of starch on white shirt collars.

She'd invent songs to fill the forest
 of her basement, exchange her dark
  images for some long forgotten dream—

the high school dance, the silver shoes,
 that day at the park just the two of them.
  Her high soprano carried us both away.

Sequoias ♬ 2002 First Place Winner
They stood quietly together,
even when glaciers
scraped the Sierra Nevada.

No Sequoia dies of age;
lightning burned black rooms
into their lower trunks

where dogwood trees gather

their skirts about them.
Indians say the flutes

in their branches are spirits
escaped from sacred burial grounds,
not wood thrushes.

And these ancient groves
that shred the blue pool of sky
insist upon our ragged need

to listen to what the flutes are saying.

<u>BOB SEDGWICK</u>

<u>Honky-Tonk</u>
Music that mirrors
the emotional culture
of weekend watering holes
where Blue Collar America
two-steps its troubles away
in boisterous barrooms
that purvey the spirits
of dancing and drinking—
of loving and losing.

Music transplanted
from rural religious
social gatherings
into urban settings.
Moving melodies
on addictive tracks
that keep it reigned in
to mainstream Country
and Main Street U.S.A.!

<u>WANDA D. SIMONI</u>

<u>Piano</u>
Black, winged presence
dominating the room,
you stand there, mute,

but forever calling.

Each journey I might take now
must be measured by the taught tension
of your strings,
pulling me back with anchor weight.

I reach. . .
satin touch of keys,
on black and white topography,
familiar feel of each contour,
each leap.

What need to travel when I have the Alps
to conquer in the Chopin Etudes,
the Russian peasant
in Mussorgsky's "Pictures at an Exhibition,"
Norway in the songs of Grieg,
and a silver cup of Polish soil
in the heroic surge of a polonaise?

Outside, the seasons pass,
but with my seasons sing
with the "Winter Etude,"
Tchaikowsky's "Troika,"
or Sinding's "Rustles of Spring."

On your sounding board
not as history, but live:
Bach's contrapuntal designs,
Mozart's lacy wrought-iron elegance,
Beethoven's snapped strings,
and Scriabin's tortuous cries.

Those under your siren spell
need not grow old
as long as they can run
deer-footed over the keys,
strike thunderbolts,
and make hammer heartbeats legato and sing.

That man should have been so bold

as to have created such a thing
where, on bared anatomy of metal, felt, and wood,
he can orchestrate
all the emotions of a human being.

CHRISTOPHER SMITH

Miles Davis

That slender, violent, poetic, frightening, brilliant night-black man,
with the stance of a boxer,
the grace of a toreador,

and a glare that said
"prove it" &
"show me something new";

who always heard everything,
yet always heard beyond;

who could hear
past the present,
past the future,

to alternate possibilities,

and the stark, cold, lovely music
on the dark side of the moon.

Rilke's Bouzouki

If Rilke had played the bouzouki,

If Emerson had written songs,

If Thoreau in his solitude had learned to love collaboration,

He, or they, might have sounded like this.

And Buster Keaton with a bad back might have danced a comic ballet with his microphones,
Chaplin channeled a gypsy jazz guitarist,
Robert Frost played a few friendly fiddle tunes,
Jelaluddin Rumi sung songs alone under dripping Northwest

deciduous leaves.

But since they didn't,
Since they didn't,
You did.

The Session
Listening to a tape of a session from my old home town,

Brings it back:

Voices, the clatter of glasses, tunes half-heard, never learned,
Once lost, now found.

Old lovers, old rivals;
Old victories, old loss,

Many miles and years behind;
Sliding away like a ship down a quay,
And the turning of the years between;

Like distant voices on a crackly 78,
Or static over short-wave,

Or the crisscrossed synapses of half-remembered tunes,

And the faces of friends gone by.

JENA SMITH

Bach for Breakfast
In Preludes to the morning
you visit 'cross the table from me
butter stains the Figured Bass
of the New York Times which
Aires the subjects in world Fugues
contrasting Counterpoints.
Dark aroma nectar in our cups a
fresh "Coffee Cantata"
with Chorales that nourish give
this day our daily bread spread
with "Suites" (the English ones)

of Orange Marmalade

Clear the table after eating
With a Passion leave to seek
the keyboard's minor modes
Inventions for the daily griefs
my fingers bury in your canons
death desertion wounds
a-Massed as Organ-ized
"Toccatas" heal.

I will rise "Well Tempered"
from my Clavichord
Dear Johann
"Bist Du Bei Mir"

<u>Ella</u>

Out in the streets running numbers at 14
she spent three years in a jail for young girls.
There she would sing – Man! Could she sing!
Harlem – a talent show and she was launched.

17 on the road with a big band
jamming from coast to coast booked every night.
City to city that black woman's throat
throbbed as white's cheered – (but
don't drink from *my* fountain!)

Dusky voice pounds of her pranced as that
sound hit its target – her soul straight to yours.
A "Lost Yellow Basket" At 21 famous but
nobody loved that big Momma's fat frame
as huge as her talent as great as her love.

She was a puller of strings made the patron's
limbs twitch jumpin' jag to her jazz.
Girth shaking Ella throbbed "Blues" till they
darkened to purple and blackened the night

That voice could soar
It could blare like a trumpet
imitate any sound a horn could strut

slide valves and shake trills to
vibrate your marrow she'd
scat in a dizzying arc of sweet flying riffs.

Nobody noticed the
spotlight lit cheeks with
wet streaks as her longing
poured from her mouth.

VICKI STRINGER

Closure

I play some Mozart themes; I am infused
with reverence for their mischief and their pain;
I turn the poignant pages once again
of Shelley, Keats---my twin loves oft perused;
I stand before a Rembrandt---how he used
his lights and shades, ennobling the mundane!
But worship fades to wondering---what explains
the dead Unknown whose art the world refused?

Will people in the year 3000 view
our scribbled symphonies with admiration?
Praise our odes? Small matter if they do---
"Creating" has its own exhilaration
although our works be candles in the sun,
while Masters light the stars, one by one.

Philemon and Baucis Re-Incarnated in Iowa, 2000

For 80 years they'd lived here on the farm,
clinging to each other, arm in arm,
viewing New Age mores with alarm

They fantasized on myths of Grecian fame;
Philemon and his Baucis they became,
though Phil and Becky were their real names.

Country folk of very scanty means,
but well-informed, they read the magazines,
New Yorker, People, featuring city scenes.

And once they went to hear a symphony,

Mozart's "Jupiter", admission free---
a trip with grist for Aristophanes!

The setting is a stadium, outdoor,
where symphonies in progress can't ignore
airplanes nearing, engines all a-roar.

A thousand eyes are fastened for a time
upon the plane, whose blaring upward climb
has made the orchestra a pantomime.

The guests, urbane, resigned to heavens rife
with noise, just shrug and say, "O well, that's life,"
except for old Philemon and his wife.

To them the airplane seems to symbolize
a threat to something that they dearly prize;
precursor to more evils in disguise.

For years they'd watched with pain a world of change,
a world they wished that they could re-arrange
and not accept the "freedoms" new and strange.

Art betrayed by urine on the rood,
elephant dung, religion of the lewd;
music gone from classical to crude.

Melody, crushed in scales called 12-tone;
tuneless random beeps John Cage has shown;
Rock and Rap---but where has "Music" gone?

Poetry, mother of Rhyme, compelled to mourn
her daughter, standing in the "alien corn",
where Rhyme, so far from home, must be reborn.

These current trends, the quaint old pair agree,
burn out like novas in the galaxy,
the world stripped of its last hypocrisy.

Their vision is a 60-second flare,
flaming only while the plane is there,
but something else, a voice, is in the air:

"Philemon, only Zeus can read your heart;
and as your benefactor I will start
restoring grace and beauty to the Arts."

Philemon, dream-like, hugs his Baucis when
he says, "My dear, the plane will go and then
we'll hear the lovely music once again."

ANN TAYLOR

Fadista

Out of the Lisbon night,
we descend to soft candles,
thocking of corks, tinkle of glass,
blendings of Portuguese, American,
German, Spanish.
Determined forks scrape
laden clay plates.
Twirling my wine-stem,
I lean back, at ease.

Guitars, spotlit, edge in among us;
Cigarette snuffed, she follows,
with inky hair flipped, teased tremendous,
dark foundation ridged deep,
eyeshade turquoise, lips red -- the sauciest hues in the room.
Her jet-sequined dress hugs sharp contours.
She breathes deep, one hand to her stomach,
painted fingers spread. The other tugs
black shawl tight over angular shoulders.

In the hush, she squeezes eyes shut,
cries out smoke-darkened notes.
I secure a grip on my wine glass,
nudge my chair back, away from center,
but feel walls pressing in,
keeping the space far too small.
They say her song is of loss, yearning, cruel fate.
I attest to the sure assertion of passion
arrowing straight through us all.

ERIN ALAN THOMAS

Voice
Presently
I struggle
To develop my voice
One day at a time
It is a welcome struggle
For it is my voice
That stands
A great representation
Of mine heart
There are days
Times
Where I can sing
Without effort
Hardly a thought given
Clear and resonant
Filling all the air
With the sound
Of mine heart soaring
In unbridled expression

Other times
My voice
Draws within
Barely able
To find release
I'll sing…
The songs of mine heart
But mine heart
Instead of soaring free
Seems to crash
Hard into my throat
So that my voice
Fragments
And great strain
Torments my efforts

Yet…
I have learned
This should not be

There should be
No effort
When singing
Just a lightness
Dancing forth
From mine heart
Through my voice
Into and beyond
My thoughts
And so…
I endeavor
Daily
To let mine heart
Find its freedom
Lightly floating
Free and unhindered
Along my spine
Through my thoughts
Up to the heavens
And letting go

PEARL MARY WILSHAW

Piano Duet
Musicians,
wed to a common instrument,
sharing ties, bonded by
key and time signatures
alternate dynamics and touch
in response to nuance
or color, even as fingers
skillfully weave delicate,
spider-silk threads,
tone over tone, under and
amid webs of emotion, whose
fragile hues intertwine
melodies transferred hand to
hand, partner to partner while
sharing dominance, sustaining
rhythmic accompaniment. . .
individuals performing ensemble,
completely selfless.

ACKNOWLEDGEMENTS

Elizabeth C. Axford (Del Mar, CA): She received her MA in Musicology from San Diego State University in 1995, and BA in Music from the University of Illinois, Urbana-Champaign, in 1982. A studio piano instructor, she is the author of *Song Sheets to Software - A Guide to Print Music, Software, and Web Sites for Musicians* and *Traditional World Music Influences in Contemporary Solo Piano Literature*, the multicultural repertoire guide for pianists. Other publications include *Merry Christmas Happy Hanukkah - A Multilingual Songbook and CD, I Practiced! I'm Proud!*, and *Pieces for Piano*. She is co-author of several children's books on music. She is a member of ASCAP, NARAS, MTNA, SCBWI, TI:ME, and NSAI, for which she serves as the San Diego regional workshop coordinator. A composer, songwriter, and arranger of piano music, her "Keyboard Chops" articles can be read online at www.Indie-Music.com.

Dr. Ronald K. Burke (Sherman Oaks, CA): He is professor emeritus of Speech Communication at Syracuse University and a free lance writer residing in southern California. His three published books include *Samuel Ringgold Ward: Christian Abolitionist, Frederick Douglass: Crusading Orator for Human Rights,* and *American Public Address: A Multicultural Perspective*. Other publications include articles for academic journals and poetry. His poems have appeared in *New Mirage Quarterly, Poet's Corner, Blue Collar Review, Timbooktu Online Journal, Mayhem Publishing Online, Tucumcari Literary Review, Raskolnikov's Cellar, Melting Trees Review, Clark Street Review, Nomad's Choir, AIM, Thorny Locust,* among others. "In Jazz There is Unity" appeared in the *Haight Ashbury Literary Journal,* Vol. 19, #1, 2000.

Marianna Busching (Walkersville, MD): She has been a compulsive writer since age seven. She is a serious professional classical singer who is winding down a career after having appeared in such places as Carnegie Hall and the Kennedy Center. She is on the faculty of The Peabody Conservatory. She won a Poet's Award at Converse College and has been invited to read her poems at Border's. The latest of her poems to be accepted for publication include "Supper" by *Living Church,* and "Songs from the Couch I and II" by *Mausoleum*. A Washington composer set five of her poems to music especially for her voice. She premiered them at the Renwick Gallery in Washington, D.C., and they have been performed frequently since.

Stephen Butterman (Ypsilanti, MI): He is currently pursuing a Masters degree in creative writing at Eastern Michigan University. He has published two nonfiction books on bicycle touring, one with Wildreness Press, the other with Anacus Press. He has published poetry, essays, and fiction in several dozen publications including *Immaculate Cauldron* and *Cornfield Review* (two literary journals of Ohio State University), *Inland, Baja Times, Wyoming Rural News, American Gardening, Hartford Woman, Paperback Parade, Atrocity,* and *Catholic Forester*.

Loraine Campbell (Seattle, WA): Her poems and short stories have appeared in *Grit, The Sun, Chrysalis Reaer, Aim, Writing for our Lives, Works and Conversation, Potato Eyes, Sweet Pea Review, Papyrus, Pulse, Chiron Review, Circle Magazine, Struggle, Dana Literary Society, Hard Row to Hoe, Bellowing Ark, The Awakenings Review,* and *The California Quarterly*. "Silent Way" is from a self-published chapbook titled *Marooned.*

Fern G. Z. Carr (Kelowna, BC, Canada): She is a musician, lawyer, language teacher, and past president and director of the local Society for the Prevention of Cruelty to Animals. Music is an integral part of her life. She has given private piano lessons, served as an accompanist, and taught choir at the high school level. She plays the piano every day and enjoys singing and performing with a university choir. Her poetry has been published in Canada, the USA, England, Wales, and Australia. Her publication credits include: *Canadian Writer's Journal, Thalia: Studies in Literary Humor, Green's*

Magazine, Writer's Guidelines and News Magazine, John Milton Magazine, Jewish Women's Literary Annual, Once Upon A Time, FreeXpresSion, Time for Rhyme, SPCA Connection, Dream International Quarterly, VQ Online, Gentle Reader, Krax, and *Candelabrum.*

Todd Cecil (Nashville, TN): He is a UNC Chapel Hill Graduate. He is currently a musician and songwriter in Nashville, TN working on original music featuring slide collage guitar with emphasis on lyrical content and performance. Song clips and further information can be found at www.toddcecil.com. His publication credits include "Buicks" in *Penmanship: A Creative Arts Calendar 2001,* "Raising Perfect" and "Kiosk" in *Way Station Magazine 2001,* and "Next" and "When She Writes" published in *Offerings 2002.*

Laura Cobrinik (Boonton Township, NJ): She graduated from Caldwell College (magna cum laude) in May of 1988. She is a former member of Women Who Write in New Jersey, and is now a graduate student at The Palmer School of Library and Information Sciences, Brookville, NY. Her other works of poetry have appeared in *Interface, The Delta Epsilon Sigma Journal, The Storyteller, Library Mosaics, The Jewish Woman's Literary Annual, The Quarterly of The National Writing Project & The Center For The Study of Writing and Literacy, Manna, Haiku Headlines,* and *The Aurorean: A Poetic Quarterly.* Her poem, "If Emily Dickinson Was Jewish," won third prize in the National College Poetry Contest, 1996. She has also been published in the "Chatter, New Jersey" column of the New Jersey section of the *Sunday New York Times* on numerous occasions. Her poems have also appeared in the Spring 2002 issue of the ALA/ASCAL journal, *Interface,* and the December, 2002 issue of *TheAurorean: A Poetic Quarterly.*

Deborah A. Dessaso (Washington, DC): She is a native of Washington, DC and a published writer and poet. Her essays and poems have appeared in the *Washington Post,* the *Washington Informer,* and several local and national literary and small press publications including *Obsidian, Parnassus Literary Journal, Writer's Exchange, The Mage,* and *Dialogue.* Her poem "The Tuning" was previously published in *The Aardvark Adventurer,* April, 1998.

Jim Dewitt (Deceased): An educator for over thirty-one years, he taught Language Arts from the elementary to university levels. He also authored linguistics textbooks. Over 2,000 of his poems and writings appeared in various publications, including journals and university presses, throughout his writing career.

Gelia Dolcimascolo (Atlanta, GA): A former modern dancer and the daughter of a concert pianist and composer, she is currently a writing lab assistant and facilitator of The Writers' Circle at Georgia Perimeter College in Atlanta. She has taught creative writing through the college's Continuing Education Division. Her poems have been published in *Poets, Artists & Madmen, bluemilk, Dancing Shadow Review, Mediphors, The DeKalb Literary Arts Journal,* and *The Atlanta Journal-Constitution.* She has co-authored two poetry chapbooks, *Adagio* and *Encore!*, and is preparing a collection of her own poems. Her poetry addresses familial and personal relationships through the arts. "Danse Poetica" was previously published in *Adagio,* 1997.

Mary E. Duncan (Greensboro, NC): She is a poet and author of children's stories. She also writes songs for children.

Elaine Erickson (Urbandale, IA): She is a composer and a poet, and teaches piano in her home. She has five books of poems published by Chestnut Hills Press in Baltimore, MD. She has previously been published in *The Maryland Poetry Review, Briar Cliff Review, Opus Literary Review, and Lyrical Iowa,* among others. She won first place in the Barnes and Noble Contest in Des Moines, IA in April, 2003.

David Fagen (Deceased): He was a retired attorney who enjoyed creating humorous satire. He considered himself the illiterate man's Jonathan Swift. He played the flute, specializing in the Baroque scores of LeClair, Blavet, Naudot, Stamitz, and Corelli. His nephew Donald Fagen is of Steely Dan.

Mardelle Fortier (Lisle, IL): She has won many contests in creative writing. She won two contests recently in *ByLine Magazine,* one for poetry and one for fiction. She has about sixty poems in print, in journals such as *Chicago Literary Review, Rhino,* and *Piedmont Literary Review.* Some years ago, she was an assistant editor at *Rhino,* and is now a poetry editor at *DuPage Arts/Life* published by Benedictine University. She teaches writing at various Chicago area colleges such as the College of DuPage, and has taught in colleges for seventeen years. She holds a doctorate of comparative literature from the University of Illinois. For years she has been a member of Phi Beta Kapa, and is currently president of the Illinois State Poetry Society. "Katerina Witt Competes" was previously published in *DuPage Arts Life,* Fall 2003. "Skater to *Red Violin*" was previously published in *Quantum Pulp,* Spring 2002. "Composing Poems as Music Plays in a Coffee House" was previously published in *Byline Magazine,* February, 2000.

G. G. Gilchrist (Deceased): A Brooklyn, NY native, he was published in *Armadillo/Candlelight, Timelapse, Iliad, Black Creek Review, Aurorean,* and *Smile,* among others. His poem *inexpressible is music* won an Honorable Mention in the Spring 2000 Iliad Literary Awards Program.

Howard Gold (Las Vegas, NV): He writes on the humorous side of life, on a variety of subjects, sings, and plays the piano. He has been published in the Las Vegas Chapter of the *Menza Newsletter.*

Peter Grimaldi (Broomall, PA): His poetry has appeared in the following publications: *Trains, Philadelphia Poets, The Plastic Tower, Poetry Motel, The White Crow, The Advocate, The Oak,* and is forthcoming in *Hidden Oak, Red Owl Magazine,* and *Cleaning Magazine.* "Piano Moving," "Piano Dust," and "Music Child" are previously published, having appeared in *Fearless* and *The Oak.* He is a lifelong resident of the Philadelphia area, and he teaches language arts in the city of Chester.

Anita Metz Grossman (Deceased): She was a pianist and a composer. She performed both classical and jazz on piano. Writing about music was her chief joy. Her poem *Cadences* was published in *bluemilk.* She published with her colleague, Gelia Dolcimascolo, two chapbooks, *Adagio* and *Encore.* "Piano Teacher" was previously published in *Adagio,* 1997.

Michelle Gunning (Battle Creek, MI): She writes poetry and songs, and is the mother of three children, Sarah, Alissa, and Trey. Her poem "Reminded" won an Editor's Choice Award at www.poetry.com.

Kathleen Gunton (Orange, CA): She received her degree from CSULB. She has been publishing poetry for twenty years. Her poems have been published by *Hellas, NCR, Free Lunch, The Aurorean, The Christian Science MonitorSing! Heavenly Muse,* and *Fox Cry Review,* among others. She was nominated for a Pushcart in 1999. Her first collection, *Something Untamed,* was published in 2000. She is a professional photographer and lives with her husband.

Peggy C. Hall (S. Miami, FL): Her avocation has always been music-related (piano, organ, tenor sax). Whether playing the score in a local production of *The Fantasticks* or writing a free-verse "review" of a Graham Steed organ recital in Salisbury Cathedral, she has been intimately involved with the notes and the rhythms. Most recently, she received an Honorable Mention in the Soul-Making Literary Competition 2000 for "Keats Writes to His Brother Tom." Her diminishing-verse poem "Gus n' Us" and a sonnet were included in Sandra Riley's 2000 children's book, *The Greenbear Chronicles.*

Joseph Hart (Visalia, CA): Before he met his dearest friend, his poems were very impersonal, but have since become more feeling. His heroes in poetry are Keats and Millay. His favorite composers are Bach, Mozart, and Donizetti. He has been published in *Fauquier, Riverrun, Parnassus, Raintown Review, Ship of Fools, Adept Press (Small*

Brushes), Catamount Press (Cotyledon), Lucidity, Homestead Review, Dana Literary Society, Northwoods, Beggar's Press (Raskolnikov's Cellar), Red Owl, Muse's Kiss, Kaleidoscope Review, Offerings, Nanny Fanny, Alura, Old Hickory Review, Mind In Motion, Straight Ahead, and various other magazines.

John R. Haws (Olympia, WA): He was born and raised in California. He is sixty-six years old and busy raising his second family of two sons, John-John and Joshua. The Olympia Copy and Printing Center first printed *Poetry Book-1* in March of 1991. He has been writing poetry since his college days at San Jose State College back in 1961. His poetry can be read online at http://mywebpages.comcast.net/John-R-Haws.

Derryl R. Herring (Farmington, NM): He was born in Mesa, AZ, and left immediately for Toadlena, NM, where his parents, Charles and Grace Herring, owned a trading post. He spent his childhood on the Navajo Indian reservation, where he attended the first eight grades in a one-room school. He was often the only anglo child in his school. His music education began at an early age. His mother drove Derryl and his Navajo sister, Jill, to the Waterflow Academy sixty miles from Toadlena. There they took lessons from the Urseline nuns, with Derryl studying voice and piano. His high school years were spent in Farmington, NM, where he graduated in 1953. Before receiving his BA and MA in music education from Brigham Young University, he spent two and a half years in France and Switzerland, where he served as a missionary for the Church of Jesus Christ of Latter-Day Saints. During that time he met his wife, Michèle Dunoyer, in Grenoble, France. They have three children, André, Ariane, and Pierre, and three grandchildren. He spent forty years teaching elementary school music, with the last ten spent on the Navajo Indian reservation. He has now retired from the classroom and spends his time taking care of church responsibilities, writing, and composing new music.

Kathryn B. Hull (La Quinta, CA): She is a Nationally Certified Teacher of Piano and Theory, maintaining an active studio in the California desert community of La Quinta. She is a poet and author of children's stories. The National Library of Poetry has published several of her writings. She has been published in children's magazines including *First Opportunity* and *Young Generation*. She served on the Music Teachers National Association Board of Directors for a number of years, as well as holding significant offices in her residence state. As an advocate for the arts, music and the arts are often the central theme in her writings.

Richard Kennison (St. Charles, MO): He lives with his wife, Renee, and their children, Book, Zoe, Tea, and Nadia. His poems have appeared in *Mid Rivers Review: A Literary Journal, Potpourri: A Magazine of the Literary Arts, Raw NerVZ Haiku, Once Upon a Time: A Magazine for Children's Writers and Illustrators, Haiku Headlines,* and *The Mid-America Poetry Review,* among other publications.

Susan Landgraf (Seattle, WA): A writer and photographer, her poems have most recently appeared in *Nimrod, Kalliope, The Green Hills Literary Lantern,* and *Riverwind.* She also has been published in *The Laurel Review, Third Coast Review, Pikeville Review, Interim, A Room Of One's Own, Ploughshares, Cincinnati Poetry Review, Calyx, Spoon River Quarterly, Sun Dog Review,* and *Paintbrush*, among others. Honors include a Fulbright-Hays Grant in 1999 to South Africa and Namibia; Pablo Neruda, Society of Humanistic Anthropology, and Academy of American Poets awards; a Willard R. Espy Writing Residency in 2003 and a Theodore Morrison scholarship at Bread Loaf. In 2002, she taught PhD students for one semester at Jiao Tong University in Shanghai, China. A former journalist, she teaches writing and media classes at Highline Community College.

James Lipsky (DePere, WI): He is a retired university professor who also taught in elementary schools. He earned his Ph.D. in Elementary School Counseling, and for thirty years taught teachers and other professionals to be school and community counselors. While teaching, he loved to write poems and published many, especially in professional counseling journals. Some of his poetry hangs in the USS Arizona Museum in Pearl

Harbor and a National Shrine in MA. His song "Addicted to the Dictionary" is included on the *Kidtunes* CD by Piano Press. This song received honorable mention in the 2002 John Lennon Songwriting Contest in the children's category. He also received 4th and 6th places in the Just Plain Folks 2002 Songwriting Contest. Jim is from a large family and has been around young people for years. From these experiences, he learned to enjoy writing songs and poems.

Lisa Stokking Lutwyche (Landenberg, PA): A writer for over thirty years, Lisa's poetry has appeared in *dotdotdot, Mad Poets Review, The Tamafyr Review, Sea Change, Image and Word* (a collaboration of poets and artists, in 1994), and other literary magazines and anthologies. In 1999, she was nominated for a Pushcart Prize. She has taught creative writing to adults and teens at a community arts center since 1992, and is now working on two anthologies and a novel. She is also a watercolorist and watercolor teacher, and has been showing and selling her work for many years. Lisa lives with her English poet husband, two teens, and six pets. Her father, William Stokking, is principal cellist of the Philadelphia Orchestra, affording Lisa a lifetime backstage. Like Elizabeth Axford, Lisa is a breast cancer survivor.

Mark Mansfield (Arlington, VA): He is a document analyst and musician. He has been the Assistant to the Publications Officer at the U.S. Supreme Court, a guard on sound stages in Hollywood, a proofreader for a Christmas card printer, a theatre usher, a janitor at an art school, a night watchman for a concrete company, a telemarketer, and a gas station attendant. He received his M.A. in Writing from Johns Hopkins University. His work has recently appeared (or is forthcoming) in *Aethelon, The Antietam Review, California Quarterly, Candelabrum Poetry Magazine, City Works, Concho River Review, Confluence, Creosote, The Evansville Review, First Offense, Frank, Front Range, Good Foot, The Ledge, Lilliput Review, Limestone, Literary Lantern, The New Writer, Poetry Depth Quarterly, Poetry Motel, Poetry Nottingham International, Potomac Review, Scrivener, Ship of Fools, Tulane River, Windhover,* and *Words of Wisdom*. He was Feature Poet in the Spring 2003 issue of *Poetry Nottingham International. The Ledge Press* previously published "Für Elise." *The Bay Area Poet's Coalition* previously published "The Surf Aces" and "Wonderful World" in the Summer 2002 and Autumn 2002 issues, respectively.

David Napolin (Port Washington, NY): He is a retired English teacher, having taught in the New York City schools. Since retiring, he has been published in over 150 magazines including *Hollins Critic, The Amherst Review, Parnassus, Sonora Review, The Connecticut River Review,* and other poetry journals. One of his poems was nominated for the 1999 Pushcart Poetry Prize.

Dr. Shari O'Brien (Toledo, OH): She is a lifelong Ohioan. She earned master's and doctorate degrees from the University of Michigan and Bowling Green State University, respectively, and a law degree from the University of Toledo. She is a lecturer in English at the University of Toledo and a practicing attorney, representing neglected/abused children in juvenile court. She also serves as a volunteer for the Children's Rights Council and sits on the Citizens' Review Board of the Lucas County Juvenile Court. A pianist and dancer, Shari lives with her husband Gary and enjoys spending time with her family. Dozens of her poems and essays have appeared in such journals as *Icon, Sweet Annie & Sweet Pea Press, Poetry Motel, Palo Alto Review,* and *Piano Guild Notes*.

Hans Ostrom (Lakewood, WA): His work has appeared in a variety of magazines, including *Ploughsares, Wisconsin Review,* and the literary section of the *Washington Post*. He is also the author of *A Langston Hughes Encyclopedia*. He teaches at the University of Puget Sound.

Barbara Pelman (Victoria, B.C., Canada): She teaches English at Reynolds Secondary School in Victoria and is presently Head of the English Department. She has conducted poetry workshops at BCTELA and in Victoria. She has had poems published in the *English Quarterly,* out of U.B.C., and in *Fireworks,* an electronic magazine. Two of her poems were published in *Event* in August 2003. At the weekly Mocambopo Poetry series, she is a frequent speaker at the Open Mic, and she was the featured poet on April 11, 2003. She has recently taken up flute and drawing.

Wanda Podgorska-Russell (Fresno, CA): She teaches at California State University, Fresno, and is also an RN. She has written articles for the *Fresno Bee,* and has co-authored a book on Fresno history. Her poetry has been published in The *San Joaquin Review* and in *Flies, Cockroaches, and Poets.*

Charles Rampp (Harpers Ferry, WV): He is a high school teacher and football coach. He has taught some college English, and edited a weekly newspaper while in Seminary. He interned in Buffalo, NY. He has served Lutheran Parishs in Pittsburgh, Miami, FL, Rockville, MD, Baltimore, and Manor Parish in Frederick County, MD, where he also led a poetry group. Twenty-three of his short stories have been printed; 776 of his poems have been published in the U.S., Australia, Canada, and Great Britain. He has completed four novels. He retired eight years ago to write by the Shenandoah. He accepted interim ministries at five different Lutheran Churches in the Shenandoah Valley. He is currently serving at Trinity, Arden, West Virginia.

Ande Rasmussen (Martindale, TX): He is an award winning songwriter and music publisher (Gotcha Covered Music Publishing - ASCAP) from Austin, TX. He does 95% of his songwriting by email. He attended and graduated from the University of Texas at Austin with a BA in Finance. He belongs to and participates in the Austin Songwriters Group (ASG), where he serves as President, and Nashville Songwriters Association International (NSAI.). He has had cuts with independent artists. He is the author of the very successful Yahoo Newsgroup *Inspirations for Songwriters (IFS).*

Edwin Romand (Wind Gap, PA): He is the author of three books of poetry, *Home Fire, Macaroons,* and *Blue Mountain Time: New and Selected Poems about Baseball.* His work has appeared in many journals such as *The Sun, The English Journal, Poet Lore,* and *The Rockhurst Review.* He has received poetry fellowships from both the New Jersey and Pennsylvania State Councils on the Arts. In 1994, he received an award from the National Endowment for the Arts, Washington, D.C. He lives with his wife, Mary, and their son, Liam.

Ruth Rotkowitz (Old Bridge, NJ): She is a freelance writer and English teacher. She has published poetry in *Hopscotch* and *Shemom*, and nonfiction in *Expecting* and *The Woman's Newspaper of Princeton*, where she served as a staff writer and member of the editorial board for several years. The National Federation of Press Women honored one of her articles for *The Woman's Newspaper* with a first place contest award in feature writing. She has recently completed her first novel, and is currently at work on the second. In addition to her writing, she has taught English on both the college and high school levels, in New York and New Jersey.

Jennifer Rudsit (Wayland, MA): She received her undergraduate degree from Purdue University and a Masters in Creative Writing from Northern Michigan University. She is a Midwest girl at heart, born and raised on the shores of Lake Michigan in Northwest Indiana, recently transplanted into a strange world called Boston. She moved there three years ago and has never, ever gotten used to the traffic! Jennifer currently works in the education field to support her poetry addiction. Her poems have appeared in publications, including: *Spirits, North Coast Review, White Pelican Review, Alembic, Anthology, Sierra Nevada Review, Nanny Fanny, Small Brushes, Hard Row to Hoe, Limestone, Zillah, Free Fall, Thought Magazine* and *Into the Teeth of the Wind, The Advocate, Omnific,* and *360 Degrees.*

Bonny Barry Sanders (Jacksonville, FL): Her poems have appeared in many literary magazines and journals throughout the country, including *Blueline, California Quarterly, Ginger Hill, Hayden's Ferry Review, Kalliope, The Louisiana Review,*

Midwest Quarterly, Negative Capability, Pig Iron, Plainsong, Red Owl, Red Rock Review, South Dakota Review, White Pelican Review, and several others. She has also published book reviews, literary essays, and children's stories. She lives with her husband. "Sequoias" was published by Pig Iron in Environment: Essence and Issue.

Robert Sedgwick (Del Mar, CA): He is a retired research scientist. He currently is writing his autobiography, children's stories, poetry, and songs. Some of his work can be viewed on his two web sites, www.ussongs.com and www.poARTry.com.

Wanda D. Simoni (Sacramento, CA): A Massachusetts native, she is a graduate of Smith College and the mother of five children. She has taught English in high school as well as at colleges in Breckenridge, CO, Miranda, CA, and Yuba College, CA. She supplemented her own education with creative writing courses, and is a member of the Range of Lights Workshop in Sacramento. She has been published in forty-three journals, newspapers, and magazines, including *The Writer, The Village, Piano Quarterly, Science of Mind, Sierra Journal, San Fernando Poetry Journal, American Rose, Orphic Lute, The Acorn,* and *Reflect.* Her poem "Piano" was first published in *Piano Quarterly* in the Fall 1987 issue, Vol. #139. She begins her day gravitating to the piano before her first cup of coffee. At one point, she had three pianos in her home.

Christopher Smith (Lubbock, TX): He was born on the coast of Massachusetts, and has played blues, jazz, and traditional Irish music since childhood. Now professor of music history at Texas Tech University, he plays and teaches in Ireland and across the US. He cites T'ang poetry, Zen Buddhism, the Beats, and San Francisco Poetry Renaissance, and the colloquialisms of musicians as influences on his writing. He has published books, book chapters, scholarly articles, liner notes, and teaching materials on many topics in jazz, classical, and world music, and records and tours internationally with Altramar medieval music ensemble, Last Night's Fun, and the Juke Band.

Jena Smith (Scarsdale, NY): She makes her living as a musician. Music is not only her livelihood, it is her joy. Initially a mezzo-soprano, Jena attended the Julliard School on scholarship, toured with The Robert Shaw Chorale. She later formed and conducted The Performing Arts Society, an opera and chamber music organization in Westchester, NY. She also has conducted musical comedy on Cape Cod. Presently conductor of the chorus "Cantemus." she also teaches voice, paints, sculpts, composes, and writes poetry. She has had numerous poems published in *The Iconoclast, Sunday Suitor, Sunflower Dream Summer, The Writer's Gazette, Creative With Words, Long Island Quarterly, Northern Star, Syncopated City, Twilight Ending,* and many others. She has placed in poetry contests, and was awarded a $1,000 grant for poetry from the Vogelstein Foundation in 2000.

Vicki Stringer (Riverdale, NY): Her publication credits include *American Poets & Poetry, Troubadour, Light,* and *Amelia.* At poetry workshops within the last ten years, she has studied with Nicholas Christopher, Scott Cairns, and Stephen Dunn. She has an MA in Music from Columbia University, and is a retired professional violinist and actress. She had a long, successful career in theatre, film, and TV. She appeared as solo act on twelve major TV shows, including the Steve Allen show, and has worked all over the world. She taught Music/Drama for nine years in the NYC public schools, including all the orchestra instruments.

Ann Taylor (Woburn, MA): She is a professor of English at Salem State College in Salem, MA, where she teaches writing courses, English Literature, Arthurian Literature, The Art of the Essay, and Poetry Analysis. She has written two books on college composition, academic and free-lance essays, and most recently, a book of personal essays, *Watching Birds: Reflections on the Wing* (Ragged Mountain/McGraw Hill, 1999). She has recently published poems in *Wavelength, Mobius, Pine Island Journal of New England Poetry, Ibbetson Street Press, Tiger's Eye, Reflect, The Aurorean, Sahara, The*

Unrorean, InLand, Arion, and *The Dalhousie Review*. She lives with her husband, Francis Blessington, and their two children, Geoffrey and Julia.

Erin Alan Thomas (Willits, CA): He has lived in Mendocino County, CA since July of 1999. Born in Riverside, CA and raised in various locations up and down the coast, he has been a resident of CA throughout his life. His interest in poetry began at age twelve with a publication from Doubleday, *The Best Loved Poems of the American People*. He has since never ceased to be an avid reader of poetry. Over the years, he has developed an interest in the lyrical works of many classical poets. Aside from developing his skills as a writer of poems, he has made a hobby of memorizing and reciting poems, many of which he also sings, or cantillates.

Pearl Mary Wilshaw (Center Moriches, NY): Her background includes teaching and librarianship. The Center Moriches Library, where she is reference librarian, subscribes to many literary journals. A member of the Academy of American Poets, Southern Poetry Association, SCBWI, and NYSUT, she has had hundreds of poems published by literary journals in the United States and abroad.

The Art of Music Annual Writing Contest 2002 – 2003 Winners List

2003 - Poetry

1st Place – *Perfect Pair* by Mardelle Fortier
2nd Place – *Everything About Egypt* by Edwin Romond
3rd Place – *Bobby's Crop* by Hans Ostrom

2002 - Poetry

1st Place – *Sequoias* by Bonny Barry Sanders
2nd Place – *The Tuning* by Deborah A. Dessaso
3rd Place – *Appalachian Spring* by David Napolin

This collection includes seventy-eight music-related poems by fifty North American poets, authors, and songwriters. All poems contained herein are reprinted by permission. For more information on *The Art of Music Annual Writing Contest,* please visit **www.pianopress.com/artofmusic.htm** or write to us directly.

The Art of Music - A Collection of Writings, Volume I (published in 2001) is also available, including ninety music-related poems by forty North American poets, authors, and songwriters.

A portion of the proceeds from *The Art of Music - A Collection of Writings* is donated to Breast Cancer Research. The editor, Elizabeth C. Axford, is a breast cancer survivor.